CW00557186

The Corner of Arundel Lane and Charles Street

TONY WILLIAMS grew up in Matlock, Derbyshire and now lives in Sheffield. He has published poems in a range of print and online journals including the *TLS*, *Poetry London*, *Rialto*, *The London Magazine*, *nthposition* and *Shadow Train*. He has carried out research into contemporary pastoral poetry, works as a freelance graphic designer and teaches at the Open University and the University of Salford.

The Corner
of Arundel Lane
and Charles Street

Tony Williams

SALT

London

PUBLISHED BY SALT PUBLISHING
Fourth Floor, 2 Tavistock Place, Bloomsbury, London WC1H 9RA United Kingdom

© Tony Williams, 2009

Salt Publishing 2009

Printed in Great Britain by the MPG Books Group, Bodmin and King's Lynn

Typeset in Swift 9.5 / 13

ISBN 978 1 84471 517 6 hardback

1 3 5 7 9 8 6 4 2

for Katherine

Contents

Acknowledgements

Thanks are due to the editors of the following publications in which some of these poems first appeared: *Anon, Argotist, Avocado, The Dark Horse, The Interpreter's House, The London Magazine, Magma, New Writing: The International Journal for the Practice and Theory of Creative Writing, nthposition, Orbis, Poetry London, Rialto, Shit Creek Review, Smiths Knoll, Staple, The Times Literary Supplement.* 'The Vile Organ' appeared in *Ten Hallam Poets* (Mews Press, 2005).

Thanks are also due to the Arts and Humanities Research Council for its financial support.

Sand

From the Kalahari to the Gobi—*a waterless place,*
very large and dry like the desert's own imagination—
the Empty Quarter, from Black Rock to Death Valley,
sand's names do little for its public image,

for all it cares, grinning spitefully
as it joins with the wind to clean lost livestock's skulls
and irritate the watery eyes of workers for western NGOs.
It is its own playpit. Quick or slow, it is always shifting.

Sand ruins seaside trysts and then betrays betrayers
by lurking on scalps and between the toes
to be discovered by attentive spouses. A minor nuisance,
it is the grain of dross in every pearl. It is thirsty and fugitive.

Sand would like to meet a snarling bactrian
by which to be stamped and spat upon, and with whom
to plot the murder by asphyxiation of foolish travellers
who stray to the still hollows of its dunes.

There are more grains of sand than there are
windows in the offices of hell. It morphs
and fuses into splinters of a broken bottle
under the innocent soles of children.

It bears as anti-effort the print of athletes' straining lunges,
the end of parabolas and the limit of records. It smoothes by abrasion.
Castles and condoms, bladderwrack and crabs
have learned to speak with sand, but can convince it of nothing.

It writes messages in itself until the next high tide:
'help' and 'I love you' are both erased by the surf's bitter laugh,
and you must take with a pinch of salt sand's claim
that an egg has cooked in the time it took you to read this poem.

How Good it Sounded
after Heine

Once I had a country of my own.
The trees there grew to a huge size.
The smell of the woods sounded like laughter.
The air tasted of the earth.

It was a dream, a long and wonderful dream.
For years it kissed me in English and sang
'I love you', and stroked my head,
and though I know it wasn't true,
how good it sounded.

I Leave Myself
after Tadeusz Nowak

I leave myself—leave my body like smoke
through the gnarled and inelegant chimney of my ear,
or rise in the usual way as a spirit from the vault of my chest.

No. I leave myself. Salt leaves, or is left by, the sea,
something of old ironwork
leaks from the end of a long tool like a hoe
left lying in perfect stillness on the ground
or leaning against a gate :
where iron nails attach the iron end to the wood
seems the likeliest place for such a loss, or escape :
among the flakings of rust and spider shit.

Dogs lean out from the boundaries they guard
towards the musk I exude, exhibit, which I am,
swirling the smell of the pigs in the woods
through a nest of hay, down to a kink in the river.

I'm not there, or anywhere else. There's a raspberry bush
modestly covered in dust from the road, where yokels
carry heavy items down the road
in ten-legged, hesitant crab-step, kicking up dust :
sleepers, roof lead, a grand piano, their plans for satisfying
      sweethearts.
They happen to stop, pull off the fruit and dust it
on their sleeves, in the air, blow on its absent fire to cool it.
Their searching fingers play a little jazz medley on my branches

like a cosmopolitan priest counting rosaries,
come to the country under a cloud,
staring absently into the bishop's orchard
up through scented branches towards the open veranda
from where
the man's elder daughter disappears into the house.

He can hear her, then it isn't true that he can hear her,
he only imagines it; it's worse.

The suffocating heat under his cassock.
I sympathise madly but I am only a fruit tree
and he ignores me, kicks his heels
and pulls a dead strand of honeysuckle from the wall
with as much petulance as he'll allow himself.

From the top of the telegraph pole above him
which is
singing across continents about
matters it would be presumptuous to mention,
I can see a cloud of horsemen approaching.
I can see a haystack dreamed
in the murky cobalt of a
landscape reserved for dreams
and other untethered possibilities,
and beside it
two or three or four horses
standing placidly,
in possession of their horsey selves,
reaching down stretching their stringy ropes
taking sugar lumps, the tarts, from a man
no older than I remember—which seems rather suspicious,
a heaven I imagined when I was in a self
that seems laughable, a mere heaven. I leave myself.

The Matlock Elegies

Ja, ohne die Liebe wäre die Welt nicht die Welt,
aber Matlock wäre doch Matlock noch.

[Yes, without Love the world would not be the world,
but Matlock, of course, would still be Matlock.]

— J. W. VON GOETHE

Who, in Matlock, would hear me if I cried my heart out
at the end of a night on the lash? Half of Crown Square,
the massed crowds queuing at the Turkish Delight,
or for taxis to take them home. The ghosts of John Smedley,
Rum-Tum Billy Young's Son and Mickey Morris
scouring the streets for the sons of children they remember,
to bother and bore with their dead gossip
and stories we'll not need until they can't be found.
Traffic wardens, teachers, family friends and enemies . . .
A heartfelt laugh, of course, is all they'd give me
for my troubles; no town I know
is more sickened by expressions of emotion.
The smoke of their restrained disgust
curls up Steep Turnpike, Bank Road, drops
the wrong way down Firs Parade
and stops at Circle-K, as was, for a lottery ticket.

O my beloved Matlock! Market town
with barely a market to speak of,
my county town, my botched Eden.
Old Matlock, Matlock Green, Matlock Bank,
loop of the hated supermarket road,
the old quarry where the valley's
truculent aggression pools as sediment,
the satellites of Tansley and Elton, Winster,
Lea and Holloway. Matlock Bath,
tawdry jewel, I curse you as a tourist honey-pot;
you shadow me even unto Death. You slink

like a line of warts through the gorgeous
rock of my deliverance. A part of me
wanders forever round your amusement arcades
in an off-white polyester shirt smelling of stale teenage sweat
and a blue school tie. Another is sick in the woods.

Ah, Cromford, cradle of the Industrial Revolution!
Everybody needs good neighbours. Poor relation
in my heart to Matlock, The Matlocks, a town
so singular, so bountiful in the fruit of the soul
that it's sometimes referred to in the plural!
But rarely! Matlock, your faux castle
may not sit on an Italian headland, be owned by the cream of
        Europe—
may have been redeveloped into a suite of posh flats—
but it starred the dreams of my youth, made me feel
that every life was a fairytale. Matlock, you bitch,
you deluded me. Your cinema has closed down. I love you.

Matlock follows you like a dog. You move away,
fall in love, get some perspective on the place. All of it helps.
You visit, it seems to mean less and less. Always
you carry Matlock with you, inscrutable, useless, undeniable.
Its denizens claim to know what you mean, then take their drinks
and sit elsewhere, mock you and your city fancies.
Matlock your sweet curse sits across my back.

For My Brother

The wall falls quicker and stronger and blanker than I can gesture love,
or having gestured, clarify the sense.

Walk with me along the sunlit road.
There are fewer roads and fewer walks than once there seemed.

The Rubicon

With luxurious dignity at a small table we played
piquet, klabberjazz, bezique. All good Scrabble words:
    the entropy of culture into form,
    to use an expression you wouldn't.

The *goods/not goods* that puzzled passers-by were not
value binaries but correctitude
    as the flowering of love, high-church
    quietism in a house of books and clocks.

Your heart stirs silently over another volume of Scott
as we age together at that great fixed distance.
    To find you enjoying *Schweik* is the same as reading it myself.
    We meet at weekends for our rituals—

drinks, an elaborate hand of cards, a walk—
and scan the local rag with professional scorn,
    totting heady sums of typos, or 'literals' as you,
    with your fixed Fifties English, insist on saying.

Gawain and the Green Shade

Over the river, on up the hill,
up past the circular house of the witch,
through the thin street to the top of the road
where the track runs down, and the old house is.

Away from the firing range of the soul
and the box where times before time are stored
and the threads which lead back somewhere else—
up to the woods on the hill I ran.

Through the thick mud at the derelict farm,
the water-logged gate that guards this hell,
and out into fields of ungrazed grass:
I followed the line of the hedge that had gone,

and looked where the paths led over the hill,
but then dropped down to the edge of the woods
and sat on the roof of a cavernous hole
and waited there for the man to come.

I watched the rabbits in the evening sun,
gave the strange trees new names. I had
no time for learning the strangers' names,
no love for the round house, end of the road,

the river, the place where I was young,
or the gate, or the track, or the ghostly farm,
or the viscous mud or going there
or the villages tucked on the sides of the hill

or the rabbit alert, facing the darkened wood.
I sat in the end of the sun, and time went by
as I waited for him, and the field was bare,
and the rabbits gone, and time went on.

The Lame Dog at Monyash

Its black unopenable door
is what the village really thinks.
Virgil's native name sits on the plaque,
licensed to bid your welcome nixed

to afternoons of Lethe Best
and tightness in the chest and neck
brought on by pressure at the desk
you work at to afford the move.

You should consider going back.
You'll never join the Us of Here,
or even Them of Over-There.
The locals all have history.

The white limestones are fixed
in ragged and deceitful smiles
across miles of saturated green
with paradisal lambs between

that bleat that things are looking bleak
and maybe you should ask your kids
about the role of revenant.
Leaving, you pass the desolate farms.

Their huge prefabricated sheds
proclaim the names of local firms,
contain fence posts, rusting plant,
oil drums, doomed livestock.

Landscape for August Natterer

Two darkened semis
blue eyes blazing

Malcolm and Sarah and
Chris and Leslie

staying up to watch
the final of the swimming

The Town of K., in the Province of M.

How to render it, then, the old bank's
neoclassical façade? The thump
and swat of raw materials, the hardhat suit
peering along the roofline counting pigeons,
syllables. Coming past it in the rain,
a grid vanishing quietly in the fumes
till the lights change and you swing on and out
to see it staring after you. Scotch eggs, bald-
headed clerks aswim in lunchtime alcohol,
scribbling lists of burial goods, their own—
Potter and Hart portray them as humble, caged
and dessicated sparrows—the dusty hope
that all large buildings squash and cherish. But this
is no waxwork frontage: the Two Ronnies
can be involved at some point, if they like,
and cheaper cuts wrapped up quaintly in paper
can do the rounds as currency to delight us
with the queasy air and bring to froth
the town's fat-man commerce, a meaty yeast . . .
Look at that girl walking in front of it: her hair
sends out wisps to tease the stolid columns,
stands blonde-white against the black windows.
They swallow the light that's been released from prison
and flings its sad radials towards the open
doors of alcohol—something to scoff at,
wastage, occluded ore in the local rock.
It's a valley of names. A sudden storm
dashes the may from the trees before its time.

A Missing Person

Where else do people start to look
for their loved ones but in themselves?
The nip to the shops, the route to town,
a place they stop with the wheelie bin
and just *look* and think of somewhere else—
the rhododendrons in the park,

the alley where you might have been
wherever you were going, why,
and who to meet; and then they think
of the jeans you might have worn, the pink
T-shirt and what its slogan, *I
Don't Know You*, quite what that might mean,

and while they're rummaging upstairs
to see what's dirty and what's clean,
which of your things are indispensable
and still there, they start to wonder where
you'd go if you were you. Or run,
according to the sort of trouble

you were in. And then they think
obscurely of the hardware shop
whose awning shades the silent street
below the town hall's hulk of soot,
grandfatherly advice, the stink
of metalwork and rubber clips,

and how from there a path might drop
between a graveyard and a gritstone wall
towards the centre of the place,
the domes of cobbles on the slope
pressing their feet, an infant school's
high hubbub out proclaiming peace.

A laughter in the local accent
floats across the pond. They sit
till nightfall at the swings' stilled
pendulums, watching a face concealed
by sky and mortar, stone and light.
I'm here, you say. *The town. I'm found.*

Notice of Death

Call in the council's legions to assist
in the great removal: send wagon and dumper,
dog van and red appliance, extant bus
whose passengers are late and cross, artiste
deserving of support and hospital driver,
cart from the sodden municipal course.

Send solemn alderman murmuring sweetly,
coughing director, unkempt registrar,
send nurses and doctors and carers and bills
and troops of out-contracted cleaners, and dealers
in furniture taken in lieu of rent. Send money.
Enter the data and confirm in gore

where sent and by what means the box in question,
obtain a letter from a Personage, and throw
a final number to complete the sum.
By this the heavy edifice shall *know*.
And at the signal take your place, sit down,
and listen in the echoes of the room

for something of the piece's closing chords
decaying to entreaty to be heard,
occluded by the weight of whispered lies,
the scrat of pigeons shifting on the roof,
or for that matter the offensive sigh
a youthful officer lets out, a cough,

like earth upon the blank-brassed lid,
a folder's flap when thrown down on a pad
echoing in the institution's ears
and yours also, who share these corridors
although you are mistaken what they prove,
and falter when you're told it's time to leave.

Your shoes squeak. The smell of fumigant and dust
attends your walking, and the light is drenched
in windows shaking in a rumbled gust;
the sky smells cold and clean, is vast and blanched
above the railway bridge's blackened pit
and on the dais of the steps you wait

—as if you'd left a friend inside a bar
to walk the city in the sober day—
before you join the stream, but don't know why:
perhaps it has to do with what's been done,
the thought of yellow weeds down by the car
bowed low in this incessant rain,

the radio, the engine's failing wheeze.
You think of letters which will be posted still
and how you'll cook a meal, and entertain
a day with no appointments left to fill;
books you've yet to read; the damascene
that bathes the stone slabs of these premises.

The Civil War

A church clock static on the midday chime:
the valley breathless like a desert bowl:
a boy shy in the lane in a too-big suit.
My brain no longer resists this stratagem,

but lolls instead in the meadow of its crime.
Off-shore the mackerel, blank in a huge shoal,
are the reasons my mind's land is destitute.
Under the harbour's calm I cannot see them.

Vertically the cloud builds over a parkland lime
which hides the idea of Charles I in its giant bole.
The cloud is the vision of republicans. Absolute
blue surrounds that shifting diadem.

Great Edwardian

A cock-pheasant on the steaming muckheap:
Prospero admiring all. Those deep inks,
the bludgeoned, sexual midnight and a pope's

vermillion, are his interiors. He stands,
coat-tails trembling in the breeze, and smokes
and gazes out across the wooded sea.

Mock-Tudor dragonfly, he delays his flit.
Behind him are the lit boxes of his ease,
where guests and sisters sit and wait.

His mind is gaslight. His gaze travels over
the flocked regimental walls, the farm's brickwork:
it seems as if he is about to speak.

The meal is ended. Watching the evening droop,
he hears the clearing of the plates, the tinkle
of a pianola, stubs his *Rey del Mundo*

in a jardinière, and puffs his breast.
A cloud-mass dulls the sheen of his regalia.
He shivers: his island has grown suddenly cold.

The Vision

I see the boy shocked white
in the dank mandorla of the pond,
his suspended fall, young and alive
at the point of recession into death.
He my friend: splashing into the past,
the waters lurching greenly over.

The Fence

Great storms bring sorrows great and small
— JOHN EVELYN

No one died. But an old fence falls
that stood crookedly for years, or leant
against a post fixed in crumbling concrete
for support, yawned through winters, wore
green velvet and a mist of spores
on the soft-biscuit panels, which the snails
had chalked with the diagrams of decay;
and when it falls, the boundary must be marked
with fresh wood nailed securely up
clean to a square post, new and straight,
that lets no wind or foxes in, and speaks
more proudly of the garden's state, absorbs
its creosote three times a year, but can't
remember what was here before, or grieve
for the sickness it replaced; and this
is sadness of a sort. What's blown away
is on the wind, stays only in the mind:
a man leans on a broom and stares and sighs
at the lost power of the departed storm
whose cooled passion reminds him of his own,
and tidying the broken spars and leaves
scattered across the sodden lawn, he knows
the clearance must be made, but will destroy
dormancies he cannot help but mourn.

The Corrugated Soul

The corrugated soul is always having to be patched
and is probably considered an eyesore.
The noise it makes in the wind
is hardly dignified.

The corrugated soul is a figure of speech
as a house is a figure of bricks,
lengths of timber and reinforced glass,
and a shed is a figure of corrugated metal
and plastic sheeting.
(This is why the shed
is the corrugated soul's spiritual home.)

But it isn't so much a gestalt
as a mere aggregate—
specifically, a pile of aggregate
turning moss-green under an oily rag.

The corrugated soul is not available in the shops.
Its badge is a *rodent couchant*
under the floorboards of the bower of bliss,
and any knight that didde presume,
his earhole was yclipt.

The corrugated soul feels pity without sentiment,
loves without sentiment,
considers the slope of a bitumen roof
without sentiment. That's the theory;
in practice, sentiment always creeps in
through a flap nailed down too hastily.

The corrugated soul brings no earthly benefits.
It is scorned by vicars
and New Age evangelists.

These days the most technologically advanced
souls are manufactured by Mitsubishi;
but all the main brands offer souls
with aircon, drinks holders, polaroid glass
and double-sided DVDs.

The corrugated soul has no such conveniences.
Draughty in winter, in summer
it becomes listless and demands alcohol;
but at least it can't be sold at a profit,
and the constant attention its upkeep requires
fills the time and makes your fingers dextrous.

Pressure

A procession of whales gliding under the street:
their exhalations spume startled rowans
from a litter of tarry gravel, twigs and compacted earth.
A pair of dotted lines on the archived plan—

alternating with grassy dashes that are mown
more often than the meadows they conjure,
strings of Morse banalities between road and pavement—
recessed a metre from the sleepless streetlamps,

they leak organic matter into the smokeless sky,
bunches of stunted ruby grapes hanging back
like the fruit of ignorance, chandeliers in the halls of Hades.
The light they shed reverses polarities of conscience:

neighbours, generous, concerned, close their curtains on incidents,
absolved by all these linear civic patterns—
double yellows, kerb height, angles of camber,
the faux-irregular arrangement of gables.

It rains, on and off. Leaves and sap and aphids and putrid berries
cover the cars parked neatly down one side of the road.
The local stray trots down the middle: cautious, recalcitrant,
it barks responsibly when a back door slams.

Bus Between Towns

Verges of clearways, flora and *weltschmerz*,
the waver of lane-marks, veering sliproads,
emergency telephones the colour of orange chewits,
ghosts on the bus and the chirp of their mobiles,
pornography and fox-furs striped with rubber,
signage naming destinies, and sergeants
getting relentlessly demoted into junctions.

A Lowland Palsy

This region's afflicted by the Mind of its inhabitants:
behind the breezy kitchen stands an empty window
    stocked with dolls,
    the half-lives of abandoned dreams.

Stores of glass-eyed malevolence haunt
their midnights and their waking too, divorcées,
    alcoholic couples, young families,
    high-minded and emotionally dangerous.

Their sparse dramas flee the rain and sicken
for lack of motile air amid the cooking smells and easy chairs,
    surrounded by miles
    and miles of friendless arable.

Everyone ends up on their own, prowling the concrete town
in their shapeless sweaters, rehearsing reasons for failure and for
    hope.
    Liberal but desperate, they pair off
    with their reduced ambitions,

start afresh, leaving the empty house behind with its
bad memories, drains, unsourceable Welsh slate
    and the usual sad unfinished novel
    silenced under months of snow.

Tenebrio

Tenebrio, the fabled Panther, Reynard, local kids,
a dangerous prowler—or just the usual drunk on the skids—
slipping in and out of your names and costumes nightly,
you come around here, rifling bins, screaming your vixen cry,
playing your games, leaving a guano of gum in the bus shelter.
    The mystery caller that made the dogs bark, the lateness of the hour,
    the sweet spliff fumes that rise through the air,
      backlit orange, behind the privet—you're gone, never were,
      remain in the bushes as a pair of evil stars,
when some gracious shivering husband stirs
and comes with a torch and pulled-tight dressing gown to see.
Plodding back, he hushes his wife but is awake instantly
when the floodlight's triggered by your shadow's tail,
and is taking *Nytol* when he hears the clatter of disturbed metal.
    The next day there's just a smudge of feathers and two
    twigs lying crossed in the path. Next door's window
    has been tampered with: the tracks lead to a high fence and stop.
All those night-time incidents: you move in rumours, stalk and drop,
accost and flash at the elderly and the young
and fade like the Cheshire Cat, leaving a fleshless dong
and a funny turn or tearful scream for mummy.
    You are a ninja dissembling into the bough of a tree,
    and now stand huge and awful by the wardrobe shelves,
      fixed in a rictus of mockery and wrong intent till that too dissolves,
and you depart, drifting across a city of bad sleep and prints on window-
    sills,
finding sport among its bedroom hells
and day-forsaken alleyways, lurking behind the silence:
    something and nothing, all the false alarms that diffuse
    through foolish laughter, all the violence that goes
    unreported or is shelved for lack of evidence.

The Winter Silage

It squats in a landscape of walls gone green with lichen,
honesty's paper moons ragged like burst bongo skins,
draughty hedge-holes, streams of degenerate ice,
and sections of concrete pipeline
stacked
neatly nearby in arrested quagmires.

In the lee of a cavernous sheet-metal barn,
by a breeze-block cow-shed, which emits
the usual moo and moan of that sad species,
it trickles its sluggish business like a licit still.
Bald tyres weight it down with memories of roads
and everywhere white clouds
rise from what is warm or alive.

Under a plastic cape which cracks sometimes in the wind,
the grass pickles and stinks and waits, and sometimes entertains
itself and the empty yard with its field of whispered secrets;
and sometimes the cows, too, listen, and hold their cud;
but Kine is a purblind language,
and the mulling conclave's dicta sound to them
like the teasing scent of a neighbour's trough
or a lumbering bull.

The steam of their stamping lust
sours the thought of wood-smoke
drifting down the valley, and Farmer Giles,
a capable husband but a rotten interpreter,
hears nothing of either
but the swish of the cows' tails
telling of markets next summer, and the wind,
rocking the barrow's ropes with its ghostly whine,
a dirge for the passing of his mother's eye,
outdated field systems, the ethics of hares
and the last repairer of man-traps in his sphere.

He guards the captives he has gathered, and his nose
wrinkles at the horsey smell of parvenus to the east.
Her he could cover, once a season. *He* should be shot.
The children he imagines absent, or silently contrite,
or borne of his own dry bed, whose forgetful warmth
he has known too little in the dark mornings when he rises,
in ageless summer evenings when the parish tups,
and through the nights of his wordless vigils when an owl
flies out of the moon to make its appalling noise,
circling at the edge of creance, and he dares wake no one.

His dump of feed is dynamite. The gas in the silo grows.
Carefully he unwraps the slice of cake his wife has made,
listens to the worms beneath his feet, and broods
on lay-bys doggers use on summer nights.

Reproductive Behaviour of the Dark

The dark began as gloaming miles from here,
mutating moss that spread in corridors
and dusty passages of history
before it shadowed you, priming the cough
of a delicate clerical constitution
that runs to the abbot with its find, who frowns—
and the dark is free and abroad in a new country.
It has travelled in storms over the sea (men drowned)
and over the mountains under the carriage's axle,
has stewed in a dungeon under architecture
of buttress and steep gable and impossible arch,
which moods it puts into a tragic metre,
astounding the populace, who are foolishly pleased,
then asks its Fausts to die in foreign holes
where it also thrives, lining the jugs
with the undrunk, listening to what's unsaid
and hopping into bed towards dawn
to propagate itself and roam the sullen days.

It's your illness makes you think these things.
The dark's the nearest thing there is to you.
It comes in on bad weather, is only
on longwave and was on song that date when drinking
and a night-walk under winter trees
brought matters to a head and magnificent
ruining scenes proved the dark's involvement
in the moorland, which you always suspected
and thrilled to in your more criminal
moments. It shares a burrow with the lizards,
and ventures Fridays to the valley bottom's
empty heart, the mill, whose phantom clanks
are the dark, laughing. The drinkers stand with their chips
in the fog that surrounds them as a constable holds

the danger with his torch, turns on
the patrol car's headlights. The dark hides
in its own shadow, shoots its mouth, the dad
of a young family, breeds, and will not be told.

Argument About the Definition of Red

Dessert is almost ready, the final strawb
bulges its angry glans in front of you,
its whitening heart, a glossed womanhood
hulled and advertising, by its blush,
a sweet castrato purity that shimmers
on the tongue, all thin words, the pain
of the raw knees of youths condemned to the final bend
taken at maximum revs. It tightens,
and heaven's hoardings approach. —Which provokes
a ripple of laughter visible through the felt
buttoned over a royal belly, and up
drunk Henry's nose, heraldic pincushion
subsumed in a smell of crushed rosehips, cut
flowers, cut limbs, releasing liquid far
crimsoner, port wine of a man's own vintage
(a blushing courtier's), shade of upholstered gloom
in the haunted residence, a rare venison haunch
eaten by the vamp or weals across the backs
of malnourished and delinquent boys,
on which the heavy curtains of the house
are decently drawn. A sufferer of the clusters,
meanwhile, groans in a distant room, from where
drab peafowl can be seen strutting
the old parterre. For some reason this
makes you worried about the missing shotgun,
and as crows caw you look down upon
a miniature bunch of the true, the sourish morello
grown for the hell of it by Diablo from Del Monte,
a lone raspberry hollow on the white plate.

My Love

My love is like
a burning haystack in a civil war:
I hide in the quiet farmhouse,
imagine history running away with her.

She brightens chapters of the classics
I have yet to read.
I read them. They are only books.
No whiff of her assured perfume

tightens the biscuit smell of their pages.
She is the rattle of a closing latch,
the subject of a conversation stopped,
the cooling coffee in a room I enter.

She flies with the birds I blunder near,
nips into doorways as I cross a public square,
confides in other people, and lives in the future.
She falls through my hands like water.

A Room of Old Presses Reprinting a Great Work

Only a solid floor can take the weight
of so many words being proclaimed at once;
along a corridor runs the raucous hum,
cokehead chatter in morse, maybe a jazz
drummer and bassist going it hammer and tongs,
then down a short fast-fingered run of steps
into a basement hangar of aero engines
busy imagining their flights. And it is
music that these beasts transcribe so flatly,
the clank and clatter of black, industrial pianos,
a shadow of music, air on the play of light
in the darkness, what the mind of the quaint original
misremembers in Hell, where, finding himself at war,
he's struck by a squadron of stalled tanks, their tracks
shaking and shells ticking with the sly menace
of pamphlets dropped from above. Enigma
machines, their fonts baptise in ink
the bright thoughts' impossible expression,
unlocking with a full array of keys
that which once said is heard and heard again
across years and continents, as in an orchard
where the muted evening sun recalls
the print-room's seedy yellow lamps,
the text modulates gently inside a reading voice
and a cat negotiates a glass of wine
set down by the foot of a wicker chair,
far from the bang and stamp, hot metal and grease,
the smell of the sheets' lost virginity
and the overseers passing about the ranks
in dreadful search for jams and the one heroic typo
probably perfroming now its word against authority,
off-kilter as the rest of its atomic gang of glyphs
beat out the drums of the tribe, barbaric to the ear
but, understood, a psalm of beauty repeatable.

Poem for Tuesday

for James Sheard

Tuesday, you are waiting for me
just out of reach—further away than Monday,
of course, but nearer than the rest of next week.
Tuesday—with your full-tilt weekday clatter,
tendency to flash by regardless of deadlines,
and promise of dog-training classes in the evening.
Tuesday, the bank-holiday fall-back of all events
habitually scheduled for Mondays, except
the emptying of the bins, which seems to drag on
randomly across the whole of the following fortnight.
Tuesday, precursor of Wednesday with its awful
midweek finality—and rival of that day
for the transmission of European club football.
Tuesday, on which I used to have History
in the morning and English in the afternoon,
and by the time English was history I'd be
sure once again that I was in love with my English teacher
in spite of her grey hair and disciplinarian approach—
Tuesday, in whose early evenings
I ran home to masturbate joyfully
with the after-images of Miss Pearson
and Eustacia Vye fresh in my mind.
Tuesday, irreproachable day,
your morals and the sound of your name
are both sweet beyond measure. Who would have thought
you were named after the god of battle, or that he
would have his hand bitten off by an enormous wolf
and be cuckolded by a fish of mischief?
You, Tuesday, would never
commit fornication outside marriage.
Your modesty does you credit.
I imagine you as a vicar's daughter in a floral dress,
but don't let that put you off. Bread and butter of days.
Excellent day for appointments, harvest time at the desk,
Tuesday, you are truly one of the footsoldiers of Time

and your position in the ranks makes you likely to coincide often
with my gentler pleasures, such as a couple of pints
with a friend, providing the ambience is not blighted,
as it occasionally is under your auspices, by quiz night.
Tuesday, I roll grumpily into your mornings
without comment, O inferior cousin of the weekend
and day marginally to be preferred to drear Monday
and Friday-imitating Thursday. Tuesday,
the love of all the world's plain brown birds
and non-flowering grasses flows through you.
Wait in your tumbledown altar while I make
the remainder of my grand observances to Sunday,
your suzerain, and slouch through the grim duties
of the day that follows, your deathly leader
whose name I have mentioned
too many times already
for those worry-warts, the astronomers.
See you the day after tomorrow—may the sun
shine a little first thing in the morning
and then nothing all day, may your hours
fit together somehow into the regulation twenty-four
without anyone getting run over or the Gregorian calendar
falling suddenly into disuse, may my meeting with Jim
be as Tuesday,
be as amicable and restorative as ever.

Ed Parsons Remembers

One letter after another comes tumbling out of Russia
and Gorchin's astonishing pen; I don't dare tell him
I leave them unread, in piles, for weeks, before
gorging myself on swathes of his life at single gluttonous sittings.

In June he tells me he is struggling with the problem
posed by Irrationalism. I am embarrassed
because he seems to assume I am familiar with the debate;
my next reply probes vaguely and tactfully

till he helps me out with a brief and not wholly clear
summary of the argument, its political ramifications,
and melodramatic hints at the mutual animosity
expressed in his correspondence with APF Gottfried.

By October I am seriously short of funds, and sell
all his letters to a man from the CIA. It is a gloomy autumn.
By the time the trees are back in leaf, Gorchin is dead:
I am free of his querulous letters cluttering up my flat.

The Vile Organ

Rebrakov had found an eye
—or somehow otherwise acquired it,
possibly, as I suspect, through a drunken bet,
though none of us inquired too closely.

He had had it set
in a plain box of dark
polished wood, and lined inside
in dark grey velvet, and from this

he withdrew it, slowly,
at the entrance
to the Dowager Duchess's ballroom
with the air of a man come back

to trump all the stick-at-homes
with the ladies.
Everyone crowded round to see his exotica.
It was only a human eye,

but its wet surface sparkled
as if it were a jewel. Rebrakov
said it was the eye's water,
but he did not know

how it was produced or whether
it could be called and conceived of
as the eye's tears as such.
Then some of the men, who were

displeased at the prodigal receiving
such sustained attention,
started saying Rebrakov was a liar
and the wetness was from a grease

he had applied himself,
and the eye was dead.
But Rebrakov held the eye in the air
like a conjuror demonstrating to an audience,

and said: 'It's watching you.
Be warned.
It's reading your lips and knows who
in this hall is to be called a liar.'

And he solemnly took it round
and showed the eye
to each of the people in the room,
from the Dowager herself

to the youngest and most life-cowed
debutante, and also
showed each of them to the eye.
This he did whether

they were pleased or reluctant
to come in front of his appalling souvenir,
saying the whole of Petersburg was in the room,
and in time he must make sure

that the whole of Russia was presented;
and it left a viscous residue
on the arm of a fine old Georgian settee.
Later in our cups as we talked of the teenagers

who had been led out before us that evening,
and which of them had performed and which
on the contrary had been horrified
by the violence of our stares, and how

mostly these were the ones we wanted,
Rebrakov again referred to his totemic eye,
saying it had been with him
and seen everything he had done

on his travels in the east and down
in the Caucasus, and he was glad
it could see but not speak
because it would be necessary to indict him

for all the things the eye had witnessed,
including on the topic of young girls
and indeed the manner of its own acquisition,
if it could speak—which morbid hint

we thought more than a little salacious;
and that Rebrakov's allusions to his little toy
were coming to seem rather a bore,
and so we told him.

Metcalf's Development

after Heine

I used to kiss girls
    like a zoologist handling the last egg of a rare eagle
    like a high priest in a thunderstorm
    like a bomb disposal expert after a run of bad luck
    like the victim of a cult signing away a Subaru Impreza
        in an access of future happiness
    like a character in D H Lawrence whose earthy spirit has been
    lately awakened
I used to kiss girls
    as if my life depended on it
    as if the girl's did
    in the certain knowledge that the weight of hellfire
        and the distances of heaven's eternal corridors
        lay behind the key I was unlocking
    in the service of Love, which was synonymous with Fate, Destiny,
        and the Unutterable Unity of Mind, Body and Soul
    like Sir Walter Raleigh debasing himself at the royal hem
        as a futile gesture towards domination—
In short, I used to kiss girls
    with lies in my heart
        and fervent Truth in my callow mind

Nowadays I understand
    that kissing, touching, fondling, fucking
        have nothing to do with such abstractions
    that a symbol is a terrible thing, not to be trusted, least of all
        by a man trying to traverse the region
        where emotion and animal lust co-exist,
        and not stray too far into the former
        in his efforts to satisfy the latter—
        for the sake of his health and sanity,
        not to mention his bank balance and self-respect
    —so I kiss the girls with no thought in my mind except

the practicalities of ingress, and whether
the bar will still be serving when the kissing's done

and I don't repeat any of that naïve nonsense at all—
except, of course, where necessary,

I whisper some of it in the girl's ear

Homage to Julian Metcalf

O Julian Metcalf,
>   you lecherous old time-travelling scoundrel!
>   lothario of history!
>>   stumble of orphans across the fire's asbestos grill!
>   waster of regiments, common thread
>>   in myriad shameful episodes!
>   a wolf in wolf's clothing!

You came and you violated my brain through the ear
>   and made me pregnant with yourself—
'Tell them the truth about love,'
>   you said
>   as you scribbled an invented phone number
>   down on a scrap of paper—
>>   I lay on the bed exhausted and made you a promise,
>>   my mind addled by your gestating spawn
>   —but Truth, and *your* truth?
>   and your handwriting? Despicable!

O aspirant frequenter of hourly-rate seraglios!
>   traveller in imagined time and fictitious space!
>   friend of Ed Parsons the brass-necked raconteur!
>   childish feeler of unmediated emotion,
>   compliant agent of unreasoning lust!
>   (more sinning than sinned against, may God
>>   forgive you—should he
>>   survive your molestations),
>>>   the girl
>>>   whom you infected with rabies
>>>   sends her love.

Subject of contemptuous condemnation!
>   notorious *bête noire* of multitudinous women's groups!
>   baseball-capped *flâneur*!
>   body and genitals!

I have written to the authorities about your behaviour,
     the surgical disdain,
     the crushing of fragile confidences with a well-judged
          frown.
          I await a response.

O collapser of delicate moods and arch lyrical poignancies!
     damper of youthful enthusiasms!
     user of out-of-date prophylactic sheaths!
     It is time we listened to your denial of human
          warmth, stared into the miserable
          embers that warm your kill.

You who have travelled the Slavonic east,
     sailed in a steamer to dominions overseas
          with a cane in your hand and a whip in your satchel,
     pierced hymens in the Med and in the frozen north
          emptied your bowels, I have blabbed
               all your secrets. Forgive me.

O disingenuous parser of 'integrity',
     selective moralist, militant without portfolio,
          Deep Heat-smothered birdwatching swinger,
     vocal witness of downsides, caller of bullshit,
          sneezer in salad bars,
     putter of brown glass
          into green bottle banks!
     gatecrasher of beanfests for the business-minded!
     sufferer of the yips!
          bad apple!
     pugilistic offender of race-day decencies! I have
          retrieved your hat from the magistrate
          and roasted you a chicken. Come home!

Roadhog! Congenital swine!
     Champion of 'the boys' whom you nevertheless despise!
O sufferer of bad conscience and immoderate self-recrimination!
     jailbird of the senses, spiritual no-hoper!
     superfluous bloke!
     ubiquitous antihero of world-historical events!
     ex-husband!
O pantomime villain, you too
     have a 'right' to 'express yourself'.

By Georgina,
     by all that is hirsute and gashly,
I would rather you were here in the house
     helping with the jigsaw,
but sleep under the hedge if you must, only
take your beercans and the debris of your psoriasis with you
     when you go,
     and tell that arse your cousin
     I despise his creation—
     a churl with a rubberised finish—
     and shall return it to him
     as soon as I can raise the postage.

You've Lost That Lovin' Feelin'

Remember when we watched the sun go down in the Gulf of Tunis?
That was before my conviction for sexual assault.

You wound a trail of honeysuckle round your graceful finger.
The light of the wine glowed red in your fair-haired face.

Variations on a Form by Gottfried Benn and Babette Deutsch

1

O that we were our Tsarist predecessors.
A little clump of dimwits in a country house.
Then life and death, and tea and cards and talk
would still be something really very nice.

A landlord's agent or a simple dunce,
wig-wearing, plump, yet strong-toothed like a vice.
A peck of grain, a goose, an evening with a girl—
help yourself, old boy, we'd chortle; don't think twice!

Despicable, the sergeants and the commissars.
Preferment, justice, farming, all are vile.
We are such effective bureaucrats,
but write off-duty ditties in a lumpen style.

The arctic inlet. The woods' darkling cries.
The grave stars, huge on the rumbling tanks.
The submarine rises soundlessly from the lake.
And the shore is bleak. And always Joseph rants.—

2

O that we were the pioneers of English botany.
A scene of livewires in the Civil War.
Then *wort* and *reed* and *buttockspur* and *clod*
might be our contribution to the lore.

A leaf of alga or a massive fungal bloom,
piquant and swollen like my lady's womb.
Angel's-wing or *fly's-head orchid*; name
and name and name. But still the sense of doom.

Despicable, the walkers and the lists,
taxa, knowledge, hybrids in a vial.
It makes me sick: we play too much the gods
yet my heart stops at the sun on a sundial.

Standing water. The yet unsurveyed wood.
Tiny stars among the flowering snowdrops.
The bug squats nameless on the tree's bark.
I pin it in a drawer. And there it stops.—

3

O that we wear our Primal Scream T-shirts.
A little line of speed in a pub bog.
Then drink and sex, and pregnancy and birth
would matter less than our next trip to Prague.

A Rizla paper or a simple pint,
gassy and full in my rooted clutch.
Gulls alongside the boat, a schoolgirl giving head.
I learn 'a coffee shop' in Dutch.

Desirable, the lovers and the mockers,
daring, longing, hopefully we smile.
We are such sickly, such corrupted gods.
A geezer vomits halfway down the aisle.

The gentle harbour. The lack of dreams.
The pop stars, transient as summer snow.
We shuffle blearily towards the waiting coach
and we're ashore. And off to buy some blow.—

4

Odette, we were in our prime. Alan says so.
A little club of two in a warm bed.
Then life handed us a permanent breach
via that plump nymph you'd asked me not to wed.

I leave for Calgary or somewhere soon.
When safely out I'll make for you. I clutch
a girl on a swing, it's what I reckon by.
But we're altered long ago, and stuff. Your touch—

Dispensed my uppers and my downers,
a spare, long without hope, forlorn, I
prepare such sick, such abrupt words.
I've lived my life backwards, I realise.

Gently I replace the handset. An answering machine.
The grave stares. You bother me no more.
In my pants I sleep through the sound of the trees,
sure that this is me always. And then old Alan calls.—

Gravel

Measured in tons and millions of tons
and by the bit in millimetres too,
gravels of all shapes and sizes go to give
the driveways of this world the desired level of crunch.

This poem is to celebrate the large buildings
gravel makes possible: HQs military and commercial,
technical stations, aerodromes
and the palaces of deranged dictators;

also hospitals, institutions for the arts and sciences,
schools, utilities, forecourts of car lots. Beloved of janitors,
gravel touches rats' paws and the brogues of the great.
It lies against the bottoms of fences and shares their creosote,

rubs against its siblings but will never return to the mother lode.
Joy to the hills for their Caesarean spawn!
Without it, whither helicopter landing pads,
whither *boule*, whither proliferation of fishing lakes?

Without gravel expensive machines would lack the proper setting
for the murders and astonishments
and exhaustive algorithms they perform.
Nowadays most organisations prefer it.

Gravel hides the blood which the rain washes through it, betrays
        trespassers,
and realises locally the emptied landscapes dreamed of by centres.
It travels secretly in the treads of tyres, arrives,
exhausted, somewhere else, and disappears at once.

Each piece is unique, a snowflake evaporated
to its hidden minerals. It surrounds you,
lies forgotten in the gutter or kicks up towards the firmament.
Stone's populace divided and set to work alone,

it drowns in fish tanks and sickens
in the ballast-holds of international freighters,
lays paths around a multitude of sins.
Gravel blots out place with geology,

covers the surface with what lies underneath,
making things possible. Never the bride:
no one seeks it, but a barrow-load or two
is often welcomed. It can belong to anyone:

keep it in a wall-safe or a wet cardboard box.
Run it through your hands like money.
A single grain is enough to stall your movement,
yet has no uses. In any quantity it means nothing.

The Looking Behind Walls Club

The Looking Behind Walls Club
lost its headquarters today: it got too familiar to the members
and dissipated into their sad knowledge of the city.
It didn't make the papers. It wasn't their sort of story:

all footnote, no beginning, no middle, no end. So it ended. We stood
    around,
trying to avoid conversation, coughing, poking, looking, till we saw
    someone coming,
and hid, I don't know why, inside a disused shed, then lost
an hour or two rummaging through knick-knacks and pots of two-
    stroke.

We look for lost traces, evidence of things, stuff, items, objects,
    trinkets,
crap, phenomena, dead-end versions; mistake empty crisp packets
for the Grail's wrapper. What's that hidden down there under the
    chipboard flooring?
Bluebeard's hoard? Chickenfeed? The Treasure of the Sierra Madre?

The left and forgotten down-at-heel site of foxgloves, broken boxes,
a flat football, two mouldy canvas shoes, who knows, a stash of street
    signs
from the 1930s, is our open-air cathedral. We only ever pray for
    distances,
unknowns, new anonymities and elsewheres as habitat. Hallelujah! No
    one hears us.

Sneak down the side of the old canal, snub the footpath.
Meet me under the bridge like pottering urban trolls, or
vault the chain-link into the sub-station's gravel yard for no good
    reason,
or anywhere. Don't tell me postcodes, addresses, *la-la-la* I can't hear you.

Describe it to me. Its nameless locations, where it leaves the track,
    the shape of its nothing,
its colours of neglected grimes, the feel of moss on your fingers.
What songbirds weren't singing there. Micro-climate, geology. How
    many minutes
you wasted. Whisper it, don't write them down. Someone might use it.

This club's no fun any more. Too organised. We burn the rolls. Our
    song drifts out
one more time across a web of dusty brickwork gennels: *Don't fence
    me in* . . .
We sniff the air: corroded metal, dinners, stagnant water.
Always another wall to look behind. The unknown region slides.

The Old Harlequin

Nursery Street crosses The Wicker at its inner end, inside the sourthernmost curve of the flaccid Don where it reaches and shies away from the city centre's hump. It used to form a section of the ring road; now the area behind Nursery Street has been razed and transformed into a knot of lanes and road signs, and the ring road disdains its old route along the bank of the river.

The company I worked for moved in to the old city mortuary in the first summer of the new century; the big, empty rooms still wore the metal stubs of old equipment high on their walls, and one or two—but not the ones we frequented—had noticeable camber, and discreet canals running rounds their edges, for the drainage of blood. There was a dismal yard, in which a caravan, with no operational purpose, soon appeared and died.

The ex-mortuary lived in a row of similarly battered, oddball buildings: an obscure church and a scientific company occupied adjacent and featureless sixties blocks, beyond which a refurbished mill provided office space *à la mode* for design firms, therapists, business groups and IT consultancies. Facing the caravan in its yard was a supplier of glasses to the drinks trade; here the row curved round, via a hotel of indeterminate quality and invisible clientele, to join the glorious decrepitude of The Wicker with its stinking newsagents, shops selling fried chicken and fishing tackle, all-night chemist and the boarded-up corpses of pubs.

The pubs—The Viaduct, The Big Gun—were an index of the area's decline. We, the symptoms and observers of change, assayed a leisurely crawl on successive Friday lunchtimes to find a local and a feel for the place. But they closed quicker than we could gather the stomach to enter. *The owner of this building is hereby given notice that it will be demolished on 17th August 2000.* They never were: the notices themselves seemed to become abandoned. Those pubs not closed did a brisk trade in violence and hostile, near-Western catatonia. The Hare and Hounds lay opposite my new place of work and we watched the regulars arriving from just after ten to stand and wait for opening. One morning, arriving at work I found on the doorstep of the mortuary a bag of low-grade cocaine; another time a crowd of people surrounded a man who had been run over; such events seemed consonant with the place. At the other end of Nursery Street lies The Manchester Arms, which honourably, oddly, changed its name to The Harlequin when its rival a street or two away was demolished to make way for the new layout of roads.

The old Harlequin sat dormant among the backstreets lying in a rectangle beind Nursery Street and The Wicker. The surrounding buildings were industrial premises used and disused—and a massage parlour-cum-brothel—set in a network of narrow one-way streets leading insistently back to the ring road. So who can have been the clientele of The Harlequin I do not know, unless it were the ghosts of the old-timers who clung on in the cutlery shops. I visited it once, before it closed, but even now I don't know whether I drank there or simply peered through the windows. The entire memory is frosted; I see silence and empty tables, cigarette smoke and photographs. The men in the photographs are the men allegedly sitting in the corners; behind them you can see the same photographs, a chronological Escher. Is the bar closed or open?

I can't go back and check. Still, you can search for it on the internet. When I do so, and look at a photograph of the old Harlequin as it was, it looks bigger and more imposing than I remember, a landmark on the corner of a wide road. I want to walk behind it and find its quiet side, stand admiring it among the still and silent brickwork, wishing it could remain as it never was.

The Corner of Arundel Lane and Charles Street

Midwest tornado-hunters do not storm
  across the desert with more warmth
than I, attracted by the sunset's flare,
  fly to where it sinks, and stare
tender and dispassionate as a friend
  at what is coming to an end,
the evening of a dormant farm, or house
  untenanted and verminous.
I travel randomly by foot and bus,
  and with no data from the skies
to guide me to the gruesome, mossy yard
  by which my atmosphere is stirred,
the gulf of house-backs, broken pots and drains
  which no whole window looks upon;
like them, to satisfy my human lust
  for seeing things reduced to dust
and have my sadnesses provoked, I race
  towards the funerals of place,
and watch—and watching feel myself grow rich—
  the infill of a stagnant ditch,
then find a dirty pub and hold a wake,
  alone, and toast the world's mistake.
My fellow guests wear suits of soot. We speak
  about the state their crumbling brick
betrays. Their chimneys are forlorn salutes
  to something going down the chutes.
I thank the curve of their decline that makes
  their final moment mine. I take
the back way through the England-flagged estate,
  shin up and leap a padlocked gate
and cross the paddock where no horses are,
  the yellow grass, where I inter
the moment of the dying of the dead,
  and I am turning in the road
to catch its final flash of sun, its gasp

of clarities. If you should pass
a *Private* sign by ivy-covered cliffs
        inside a fly-tipped wood, and if
a culvert empties at its foot into
        a runnel, canalized and blue
with algae, petrol and pollutant scum—
        then call me, tell me, and I'll come
and duck the wire, stand on the concrete foot-
        bridge, fondle the freezing rail and put
a cough of benediction on the blight
        that takes its time upon the site,
for what that's worth. And when I come to die
        deserted pavements, streets, will sigh,
an iron set of steps will ring and chime,
        pretending that it knows my name,
atonal effigies of hymns to praise
        the rain, and Nowhere breaking loose.

Late Schoolboys

The speed of their gallows walk's
lower even than their backpacks,
slung pained and aslant like their
dissenting grimaces. Trudging, more

stop than start, they take long-cuts
in twos and threes through the drab bits
of scrub tacked on to public parks,
meet the dogs on their walks

and their stoic, indifferent owners. Some
lost glove rots in front of them
all winter, and they know each flake
of paint on the railings their sticks rattle.

They'll arrive in a ragged parade
that mourns into the school's façade
and wait for the worst to burst over them
in a spat shower of opprobrium.

The birch, the worn footpath's line,
the pavements and tarmac patches they learn
over years of yawns and missed breakfasts,
the dread of the official lists,

are not on the syllabus;
nothing that interests them is.
They know only the equation of day
and death, and they avoid it stubbornly,

rolling over on their lives
and bright futures as depressives.
They have their love affairs with sleep
and blush at Miss. They speak in burps.

Lateness is the state of grace
they travel through and in this place
where their dazed craniums
conceive the codas of their dreams

they daub their uniforms with mud
to make the powers storm and chide
and have confirmed that everyone
despises them, and they the sun.

In Praise of Tinkering

Retreat to the shed of your dying expertise
illuminated by a yellow bruise
    dispensed by the electric light
    warming a corner of the night,

and there with bradawl, circuitry or oil
make something other than a haul,
    the useful, profitable job
    that serves the kingdom of the glib:

astound the spiders with a welding arc
that sticks no metals and whose flames are dark,
    or flute the leg of a balsa chair
    to sit on in the house of air,

paint a still-life, a Lowry, or Mao Zedung,
spin pots or yarns, collate outdated slang
    and sling it at the dozing moon
    throughout the dingy afternoon,

rig up a web of LEDs and flex
to flash the profile of a Mazda 6,
    and snake the power down the path
    so, with a flask of chicken broth,

you need not leave the sacerdotal hut,
presenting the Master's famous silhouette
    to the watching birds, until the last
    match is stuck to *Victory*'s mast.

Produce a treatise for the gods of dust
to bless, and scholars reference, if they must,
    in later stages of their talks
    on Derby Locomotive Works,

and should the local institute request
an hour in April on the thermal vest,
    refuse the fee, but take a mic
    and eat them out of simnel cake.

Show that true alchemy's the will to make
a stilled self and a plume of smoke
    because no saleable result
    can make the maker's soul exult

like the first fizz of homebrew stout. Therefore
treat the shed to a new coat, deter
    loved ones from ever going there,
    and recollect with tender care

the layout of the walls of Antioch,
the names of kings, the world's first wooden clock,
    the rare and edifying fact
    which blank indifference protects,

and revel in the state of being apart,
considered useless: this makes into art
    the lonely, universal wink
    and order in a world of junk.

The Triumph of Orthodoxy

The local gnomes are drunk in fields behind the mist,
dreaming of Para Handy in their landlocked state.
The moonshine trickles through their karstic brains
and disappears like foxes and the dead.
    A pheasant's rusty crank's
    a fanfare for the aged sun,
    setting the dawn's jalopy
    at the duck-pond of night;
    and in the waking I set out
through pure and cold and empty air
across the paddock's frosted slope
where trees arrayed in gold leaf in the slanting sun
    are bursts of lost stars or gunfire
lighting up a frontier sides still care about.

Evergreens absorb their share of light.
Among them stands the shining gritstone of the homes,
    the yellow SALT/GRIT *staurotheke*
    inlaid with crystals of the frost that fell,
    the pylons saints astride the land,
the council building's antique town of gables
    —dreamscape hovering in a mind
    of wet streets familiar but unwalkable.

The hydro's massive side shines with the glory
    of a great exotic church, the golden wall
studded with black windows and white paintwork,
    a slab of patriarchal faith above a beard
    of hammered copper, the dessicated hedge,
framed by the scrolled effusions of the trees
beneath a stalled procession of cloud-forms
    and blueish horizons of apse.
    It is the National Autumn,

the feast of the saints of the dying year
whose bonfire is the piling on of time and season
to wood left lying in a musty yard. A diesel coughs.

So: a priesthole behind the bookcase
I had not noticed all these years.

It is as if Christmas had descended unannounced
and I'd slipped out just as the house began to stir,
the chimneys start to clear their throats
        to join their households singing.
        I think of the first bottle popping,
        glad voices and the frying of bacon,
        the slicing of pork pie and talk of cribbage
going on in a lucid interval elsewhere
while I traverse the fields along the usual lines
in shy communion with the peaceful or dying town
in the hour of its peace or dying. I think of returning

through a gold and static morning to crush
my absence from the fixed familial smile,
and try to do so, a room listening to the gentle clocks
announce me as I walk, the mist undrifting
        and birds shouting
        from tree to sharp-drawn tree.
O on the tarmac I watch my long shadow
creep from one festival to the next,
a fool in dozy Byzantium where visions of
        sunshine on stonework illustrate
        truths of old and indecipherable Greek and warm
brown-tinted windows of stuffy and idle
        Slack's Coaches in their sleeping yard.

Icon of a Bloke in Glasses Opening a Window

The
rain a golden
veil of movement
fixing things here,
the great weekday, in
a plain uPVC frame.
The figure of
a saint cum-
nimbo-kitchen-
strip-light,
dressing-gown
anointed with crumbs
and a fragment of honeycomb.
Above the right shoulder a cinnabar moth
proclaims the limited flutterings of the heart.
Above the left: a chalk inscription: *salt,*
olive oil, sugar, self-raising. The left hand's holding
a cup of strong tea; the right hand's raised to the latch
in adlocution to the sparrows hiding in the hedge.
The lost coughs and murmurs. Insinuating cat.
The 'plashing' of the rain 'upon' the sill,
and other decorative remarks;
and through a drop on the outer pane
the sky's faint light disposed into a coloured band.
The misting of the spectacles at cold air's
wet-earth-smell in-rush, the filling of the house
with spirit, the kettle containing sainted thumb
or stones from the Riding, temporary stillness,
the gold and garnet tiling of his mind.

Variation on the Fourth Eclogue

Not every song of praise begins
skulking round dingy shrubberies
in the grounds of old hotels
or walks of blushing statuettes
designed to pique the ordered depths
of municipal Edwardians;
yet these narrownesses too,
and the wide forests, breed their loves,
the one a modesty, the other
unbroken and exhaustive,
filling a horizon. Either place—
in which you find yourself alone,
hidden by leaves from the road and the eyes
of the house, at evening or early morning
(there comes the sound of running water)—
either sends gifts from the earth: ivy,
foxgloves in a clump, the white
pates of fungal monks among
habits of brown needles spread
on the spongy ground; or, coy with dust
and pale in the shadows cast by bored
cherubim staring into the distance,
an ageing rhododendron flower,
whose scent shall be yours alone. The gods
look kindly when they do not see you:
may these be the trumpets of your reign,
bluebells in the afternoon,
and miles of nameless conifers
your only avenues of state.

A Carp
i.m. Peter Reynolds

I woke to see my cousin standing there
proud of the two fat fish he'd poached,
dead and glistening on an oval plate.
One was a trout, the other something else,
more medieval but less good to eat,
eye skewed in a grimace of reproach
while browning blood congealed at the gills—
a thing unspeakable for us to share—
    and drunken laughter down the stairs
    baited our dreamfuls of despair.

Izaak Walton's Flight

Finishing a long walk along Beresford Dale
as night falls, you watch the dusk rescind the line
where air and vale meet, the local greens,
in favour of a gulf in which the brighter stars
appear to appear, and shine through soot
as signs, for seasons, and for days, and years.
The water pools, deepens, and clears its dulcet throat.
Pray silence in the snugs of Hartington's public bars
for what she promises to sing. A shiver of cold
casts over the river, a small argent and sable moth
dances ahead the length of the shadow you walk
in this aisle of country church. There are stories
you can find your way by. Remember them.
Trust to the ankle-breaking rocks, have faith,
watch as a silver shuttle moves in the water
and is gone towards its distant planet.
Wait for the trees on the hillside at this hour
to reveal what has remained there always,
what your dilating eyes would have you fancy:
a solid fishing-house, addressed by a triplet of steps
wearing scrapings of mud from the bank
of the narrow river, adorned by a gritstone finial moon
round which the universe revolves.
Inside, Izaak Walton reclines. His gurgling laugh
at not knowing anything still about fishing these streams
is the waters themselves in their icy departure apace
to the Trent and the lowland cities of mind
whose ardent confusion his temperate smile resigns
through love and exhaustion and age.
He fondles the side of a trout, whose eye
stares back in alarm with the sternness of food
before it is eaten, wriggles his feet in the leather,
oozing with mud, ripples the gills of his coat,
then stoops his head to observe
the yellow, gelatinous balls of its roe arranged by chance

in a smear on his thigh. It's the shape of the zodiac sign
of his first beloved. For her sake he retreats
at times alone off the river to sit and refrain
from lighting the candle as cattle proceed on their way
towards evening where their bells are stifled
by cloisterous air that surrounds them and he,
alone in his wet confessional, can talk to her
about the workshop domus he has made. The finnock
bucks in the bucket, and dies, but is already dead.
He would like to eat of its flesh, wherein is the breath of life.
He waits here always, and was always waiting.
He's munching his way through the plums' misty midnight
growing by day and by year to a sweet with a nub at the centre,
can barely remember the launch and celestial arc
of his beauteous craft in the darkening river.
He stares at its rocks burning white and imagines
the amethyst heavens' reduced and plunging flare
undrinkable outside the square window
on which his meditations loom,
being leisured and still at the spiral's central bulge,
an awareness of movement not wholly empty and lit
by the thought of it moving to dwell on itself in the dark.
You are only the tracks of a walker
long past or yet to come, intruding lightly
on a scene imagined through dusk's diabolical pomp
in a compact re-entry cabana of Derbyshire stone—
the walls, altar and hour and night—
with Walton inside it at peace on the seat like a throne
spinning through space and the few elemental shapes
that persist through his grief, the dim and joyful constellations.

The Flowers Singing

*I have always thought there was such beauty about a room like that, even though
there weren't any people in it, perhaps precisely when there weren't any.*

— VILHELM HAMMERSHØI

Standing suddenly, you frown down at the book
    then wander dumbly through the house,
against the muted singing of the flowers in their vases—
    an airless house of closed doors and doors
left open: jellied meats, an ox-tongue shining
    in a courtyard's steady sun, dry cushion of moss,
four glassware jars lit by rose light and by green;
    and the smell of the sea. And voices:
the house sings—a warm breath wafts through it, once,
    cools in the silence, and dies,
as if it had never been.

    The flowers' singing, strangled and airless,
recites the words left hanging in the room:
    a tired plan to interpret dreams,
a masque, the room's spatial monody
    droning on behind—everyone sitting,
recordings of music, news from around the world.
    The bons mots of dead uncles,
dated mechanical knowledge.
    Against the wallpaper whispering
a phrase or idea slides into being,
    only to hide under the dresser. The children
are bamboozled by a simple trick
    a troubled conjuror performs,
the clock retreats towards its darkness on the mantle,
    and money also is a field of shadows.
You stand at its edge, a queasy anonymous figure.
    A glass in your hand is some comfort;

the wind ignites the evening's melodies,
     and you stand in the darkening room
cloyed by the odour of flowers you cannot name.

The green and rose casts of the glass,
     the house and the singing flowers—
their songs, grandparents and their gloom
     muddled among the folk you bring in, your lot,
and other, half-familiar powers—they sing to you
     of age and agelessness, and dare you to repeat their song.
It will die in your throat. This place north of most,
     a world jealous of summertime,
its sign is sunlight powerless against the cold,
     its stone is limestone. A lamentation
animates the houses in these valleys. Flowers sing:
     the air they disturb
settles again across the words in a book,
     a phrase from a song you half remember hearing.
The house is airless.
     Looking for things, objects, occasionally people:
gloves, facial resemblances, rain and stonework
     and other rooms. They die,
and you no longer think of them.
     This house: your waking self is not a resident.